JANE GOODALL

PRIMATOLOGIST AND ACTIVIST

by Rachel Rose

Minneapolis, Minnesota

Credits

Cover and title page, © Everett Collection Inc/Alamy Stock Photo; 5, © Tom Brenner/Getty Images; 7, © ARCHIVIO GBB/Alamy Stock Photo; 8, © Bettmann/Getty Images; 9, © CBS Photo Archive/Getty Images; 11, © CBS Photo Archive/Getty Images; 12, © WILLIAM WEST, Getty Images; 13, © Steve Bloom Images/Alamy Stock Photo; 15, © Benmo/Shutterstock; 16, © Chelsea Guglielmino/Getty Images; 17, © Hindustan Times/Getty Images; 18, © CTK/Alamy Stock Photo; 19, © FRANCOIS GUILLOT/Getty Images; 21, © picture alliance/Getty Images; 22T, © CBS Photo Archive/Getty Images; 22M, © Chelsea Guglielmino/Getty Images; 22B, © Tom Brenner/Getty Images.

Bearport Publishing Company Product Development Team

Publisher: Jen Jenson; Director of Product Development: Spencer Brinker; Editorial Director: Allison Juda; Editor: Cole Nelson; Editor: Tiana Tran; Production Editor: Naomi Reich; Art Director: Kim Jones; Designer: Kayla Eggert; Designer: Steve Scheluchin; Production Specialist: Owen Hamlin

Statement on Usage of Generative Artificial Intelligence

Bearport Publishing remains committed to publishing high-quality nonfiction books. Therefore, we restrict the use of generative AI to ensure accuracy of all text and visual components pertaining to a book's subject. See BearportPublishing.com for details.

Library of Congress Cataloging-in-Publication Data is available at www.loc.gov or upon request from the publisher.

ISBN: 979-8-89577-040-5 (hardcover)
ISBN: 979-8-89577-463-2 (paperback)
ISBN: 979-8-89577-157-0 (ebook)

Copyright © 2026 Bearport Publishing Company. All rights reserved. No part of this publication may be reproduced in whole or in part, stored in any retrieval system, or transmitted in any form or by any means, electronic, mechanical, photocopying, recording, or otherwise, without written permission from the publisher. Bearport Publishing is a division of FlutterBee Education Group.

For more information, write to Bearport Publishing, 3500 American Blvd W, Suite 150, Bloomington, MN 55431.

Contents

Lifelong Activist 4
Childhood Dreams 6
Living Among the Chimps 8
Saving the Primates 16
Still Going Strong 20

Timeline 22
Glossary 23
Index 24
Read More 24
Learn More Online 24
About the Author 24

Lifelong Activist

Jane Goodall stood up to shake the president's hand. Everyone in the room clapped and cheered for the groundbreaking **primatologist** and **activist**. The 90-year-old was being awarded the Presidential Medal of Freedom—a great honor earned by very few. Her years of activism have **inspired** people around the world to protect the planet.

Jane spends more than 300 days a year traveling and giving talks to people about saving the planet.

Jane accepted the Presidential Medal of Freedom on January 4, 2025.

Childhood Dreams

Jane Goodall was born on April 3, 1934, in London, England. She was interested in animals from the very beginning. As a young girl, she would go for walks and then draw pictures of the creatures she'd seen. She also read books about different animals around the world. By the time she was eight years old, Jane dreamed of going to Africa to study the animals there.

> Jane once sat in her grandmother's henhouse for hours. She wanted to watch a chicken lay an egg.

Jane when she was about five years old

Living Among the Chimps

After she finished high school, Jane worked two jobs so she could pay for her long-awaited trip to Africa. When she was 23, she boarded a ship to Kenya. Once there, she met **anthropologist** Louis Leakey, who hired Jane to be his **secretary**. A few years later, Louis asked Jane to go to Tanzania to study chimpanzees.

Louis Leakey

Jane didn't have any scientific training. Louis believed this would allow her to study chimps with an open mind.

In July 1960, when Jane was 26, she arrived at Gombe Stream Game Reserve in Tanzania. There had been few successful studies of chimpanzees. These **primates** were usually scared to let humans get too close. But Jane tried something new. She began living among the chimps. Over time, Jane gained the chimps' trust and was able to get close to them.

Local officials would not let Jane stay in the forest alone, so her mother joined her for the first few months.

Eventually, Jane could touch and even groom the chimps.

Once Jane could get close to the chimps, she began recording their behaviors. What she learned was groundbreaking. At the time, many scientists believed that only humans could make and use tools. But Jane saw the chimpanzees doing it. This discovery changed scientific ideas about chimp **intelligence**!

A sculpture of David Greybeard

Unlike other scientists, Jane gave names to the chimps she studied. One of the first she named was David Greybeard.

Jane watched chimps use sticks to dig bugs out of the ground and eat them.

Jane made many other discoveries about chimpanzees. Before her research, scientists thought chimps ate mostly plants and fruits. But Jane observed chimps hunting birds, wild pigs, and other animals. She learned that most chimps live in communities led by **males**. Jane also found that the chimps make at least 20 different sounds to **communicate** with one another.

> Jane studied chimp body language, too. The primates kiss, hug, and hold hands in a way that is similar to humans.

Saving the Primates

In the early 1970s, Jane realized that hunting and **habitat** loss put chimps and other animals at risk of becoming **extinct**. She wanted to prevent this. In 1977, she formed the Jane Goodall Institute to help protect chimpanzees. About 10 years later, Jane left her work in Gombe to become a full-time activist. Her mission was to educate others about saving chimpanzees.

In 1991, Jane started Roots & Shoots. This program encourages young people to make positive changes for animals and the planet.

Jane hopes to educate as many people as possible.

For decades, Jane traveled almost nonstop to spread the word about treating these primates and their **environment** with respect. She wrote books, made films, and gave many talks around the world. In 2002, Jane was named a United Nations Messenger of Peace. She hoped her work would encourage people to become interested in protecting chimpanzees, other animals, and the planet.

Jane has written several books for kids. In 2021, she published a children's book titled *Pangolina*.

In 2006, a group within the United Nations awarded Jane a gold medal for her work protecting chimps.

Still Going Strong

Jane has spent more than 60 years helping animals. From living in the forests of Tanzania to giving speeches around the world, Jane has spread her message of hope for a better world for both chimps and humans. She continues her work today, urging every single person to play their part in taking care of the planet.

> July 14 is World Chimpanzee Day. This day celebrates Jane Goodall's work and raises awareness about chimpanzee protection.

Jane brings a stuffed chimp with her when she speaks to crowds.

Timeline

Here are some key dates in Jane's life.

1934 — Born on April 3

1960 — Arrives at Gombe Stream Game Reserve to study chimpanzees

1977 — Forms the Jane Goodall Institute

1986 — Leaves Gombe to be a full-time activist

1991 — Starts the youth program, Roots & Shoots

2002 — Named a United Nations Messenger of Peace

2025 — Receives Presidential Medal of Freedom

Glossary

activist a person working toward change

anthropologist a person who studies human beings and their ancestors

communicate to pass on information, ideas, or feelings to others

environment the natural areas where animals live

extinct when a kind of animal or plant has died out completely

habitat a place in nature where an animal normally lives

inspired encouraged others to do something

intelligence the ability to understand, solve problems, and learn

males chimpanzees that cannot give birth to young

primates animals in the group that includes humans, apes, and monkeys

primatologist a person who studies nonhuman primates

secretary someone who handles letters, phone calls, and other tasks for another person

Index

activist 4, 16, 22
Africa 6, 8
environment 18
Gombe Stream Game Reserve 10, 16, 22
habitat 16
Jane Goodall Institute 16, 22
Leakey, Louis 8
males 14
planet 4, 16, 18, 20
Presidential Medal of Freedom 4-5, 22
primates 10, 14, 16, 18
primatologist 4
Roots & Shoots 16, 22
Tanzania 8, 10, 20

Read More

Klepeis, Alicia Z. *Jane Goodall (Groundbreaker Bios)*. Minneapolis: Abdo Publishing, 2022.

Tyner, Dr. Artika R. *Changemakers in Activism: Women Leading the Way (The Future is Female)*. Minneapolis: Lerner Publications, 2024.

Learn More Online

1. Go to **FactSurfer.com** or scan the QR code below.
2. Enter "**Jane Goodall**" into the search box.
3. Click on the cover of this book to see a list of websites.

About the Author

Rachel Rose is a writer and coach. Her favorite books to write are about people who lead inspiring lives.